An Anthology of Poems

K J Mercer

BookLeaf
Publishing

Presentation by *BookLeaf Publishing*

Web: www.bookleafpub.com

E-mail: info@bookleafpub.com

ISBN: 9789395950473

First edition 2022

ACKNOWLEDGEMENT

For my family xxx

The Sea

The sea, the sea has an enemy
The seashore, the seashore.
It crashes and lashes and bashes
Against the rocks so jagged.

I haven't got time

I haven't got time
I told the blind man waiting to cross the road
I haven't got time
I told the begger wanting money for a cup of tea
I haven't got time
I told the crying child wanting his mother
I haven't got time
I told the old woman on the corner selling flags

Then a car hit me….
I knew that I would die if help didn't come
quickly

Help! please help!

I'm sorry, we haven't got time
Said the blind man, the begger, the lost child and
the flag seller
As they rushed on by me, on their way home.

Hull

Hull - my city - much maligned
It's people labelled unrefined
Bottom of the ratings not denied
Yes it's reputation has declined.
Yet, I feel, it's undeserved
Folks are friendly I've observed
A rich heritage has been conserved
Georgian buildings well preserved.
The city's centre been transformed
Historic dock land now restored
A waterfront to be explored
Great shopping malls so much adored
With prices that you CAN afford!
Eight museums well created
The Deep especially highly rated
Old town charm understated
It's uniqueness should be celebrated.
A cafe culture to be discovered
Hepworths arcade must be uncovered
A free fish trial can be rambled
There's parks and gardens to be ambled
Music and sporting venues much admired
A university that well renowned
The Humber bridge can still astound
Look again at Hull you'll be impressed

Its problems now have been addressed
Perhaps the balance might be addressed
With Hull now rated as 'The best!'

Lockdown

Empty Pubs, deserted streets
Behind closed doors we all retreat
Friends and family, we can't greet
Forced apart at least 6 feet
Our focus now on what to eat
Longing for that takeout treat
For online slots we all complete
Even loo rolls are deplete!
Yet house and garden are so neat
Those DIY jobs now complete
We've even learnt to zoom and tweet
Oh this lockdown's bittersweet
We praise our NHS elite
What demands they've had to meet
More PPE they still entreat
Whilst saving lives - amazing feat
We pray that Covid will be beat
We need this virus to retreat
So altogether let's repeat
Stay alert but stay upbeat!

My passion My family

My love of life is history
But not the usual kind
Not dates or wars or artefacts
That archaeologists find

No my passion is my family
And studying their past
Trying to trace my ancestors
Is a fascinating task

I've had to learn so many skills
Ones I'll not forget
I cannot use micro fiche
And surf the internet

I've gained relations in the way
Ones I never knew
And as for family secrets
I've discovered one or two!

But as I traced my family
I Discovered along the way
Poverty and hardship
Were the order of the day
I've realised now life was tough

Without the welfare state
And having little birth control
Was every mother's fate

So my study of my family
Was both unique and sad
It made me really appreciate
The kind of life I had

Who do you think you are?
Have you a mystery?
Then be like me and go and start
Your family history

Joanne

Now Jo you might well feel concern
At these folks are going to learn
For as her friend I know her well
And oh the stories I could tell!

Once out shopping you saw a dress
"That will fit me more or less "
Off to the changing room you went
To try it on your intent

But it wouldn't fasten not at all
For really it was far too small
Then as you took it off disaster struck
The dress became quite firmly stuck!

An assistant came and shook her head
"There's only one solution" she said
"Get some scissors" I heard her shout
"We'll cut the dress to get her out! "

Shame faced out the shop you had to scurry
You won't be back in a hurry
So please Jo can we definitely state
With boobs , don't ever buy size 8!!!

I guess as most of you will know
Getting stuck is a hobby for Jo
At school when teaching one day
She visited the toilet during play

But to her horror she couldn't get out
"The locks stuck " she tried to shout
No one came which was so frustrating
Knowing her class would be sat waiting
At last help but not before
The caretaker had to remove the entire door…

Then there was the time she was stuck in the
sink
What she was doing there I cannot think
Jo was sat there in all her glory
But that's yet another story ...

Now when Tony first arrived on scene
It was really obvious Jo was keen
I clearly remember her first date
She rushed outside fearing she was late

But her glasses she refused to wear
She was blind as a bat but didn't care
She opened his car door and stepped inside
"Hi sexy" she purred all dewy eyed

But then she did a double take
Quickly realising her mistake
She looked in horror at what she'd done
She'd got into the car of her neighbours son!

We all know Jo always looks stunning
Love island auditions she'd make the running
But there was just once she made a slip up
And that's when she forgot to do her zip up!

It was when she went to see The Boss
Her personal meeting with Matt Goss
He fastened her up - what a gentleman
But was it an accident or cunning plan!?

Another time she visited town
Wondering why the women did frown
But wolf whistles she did get some
She giggled and blushed a bit of fun?
But later that day
at the primary school gate
(Thanks to a close and honest mate)
She suddenly became aware
About the huge gaping tear
All day long she'd been showing her bum!
Her glittery pants shining in the sun!

But now I must stop for it's time to say
Jo, we wouldn't have you any other way

We love you dearly just as you are
You're fun and fabulous the way you are
Alright you might have made some gaffes
But thanks for giving us so many laughs!

Butterflies

Some people are like butterflies
And sometimes you may find
It's hard to catch the caterpillar
That eats the garden in your mind

But eventually the caterpillar
Must form its cocoon
From which with new wings
A beautiful butterfly will bloom.

Mask

The old man walks on, on down the street
Alone with himself and the summer heat
Alone with the breeze and the sway of green
trees
But the old man feels
Cut off, closed in, like his face ear to ear nose to
chin
He can't walk with ease because he fears a
disease.

Paper and glass

The paper world is delicate
So easy to tear apart
Impossible to truly fix
Tear stained pages
Of the book of peace
Which for us seems impossible to reach
For the people are made of glass
So easily shattered
Some with sharp edges
Minds stained different colours
That in the sun reflect on the world around them.

Once Yellow Brick Road

"If I only had a brain"
The scarecrow cried
"If only had a heart "
The tin man replied
They glanced at each other
Then turned towards Dorothy
To stare
She had a brain thinking and heart beating
- inside of her

So they turned on poor Dorothy
Jealous of what they intended to take
Scarecrow without a thought
Tin-man with no heartache

With a low from his axe
And as her blood oozed
The once yellow brick road
Was stained red like her shoes

With what scarecrow wished for
Dorothys stolen brain
His new conscience and sorrow
Quickly drove him insane
With what tin-man dreamed of

Dorothy's heart he did take
His new empathy and regret
Caused his soon death of heartbreak

And so the story of Dorothy
In munchkin land is told
The horror story of Dorothy
And the once yellow brick road.

Monsters don't exist

The human outside the closet
And the human on the stairs
And the human on the bed
Cause my little monsters tears
Hidden in the shadows
Under a dark blanket disguise
Hidden from the humans sight
From their searching eyes
Most humans don't believe in us
Like they used to in the past
We've slowly faded into myth
But some memories still last
Whispers and old stories
Even sightings from our slip-ups
But it's the children to watch out for
As we've mostly fooled the grownups
We know that if they found us
They'd return with weapons in hand
To fight us not to reason
To force us out "their land"
So under the moon and stars
When our two worlds cross over
The cycle of our fear
Will again start over
But when the young ones cry

We monsters must insist
To give them piece of mind
"That humans don't exist".

Golden Apple

For the fairest said the apple
Golden as the sun
Placed by Eris for she knew
The result would be fun
Not for them but her
Goddess of chaos
Daughter of Nyx
Rejected, left out
She sought revenge
And swore it on the river Styx.

Andromeda

Oh Andie,
your eyes bright emeralds
Your hair dark brandy
Your crimson lips
And mine with pink hue
That may never meet....
until we do
My goddess
In many more ways
Than most clear
My mind in a haze
But I'm here
At your alter
I'm here
To alter
This grief.
To pick up the cruel shards
Of the shattered life
That is ours
As I fall to the floor
The flowers in my hair do to
But the roses in my chest grow
Tinting my mind a lovesick hue
So I look up at your sculpture
The image of beauty

And love
Into your eyes
Mine fall shut
I can't wait
To see
You
Andie

I am the Sea

I am the sea
I look up
At the moon far above
I wave and reach out
But as they rise
Each crest must fall
And you remain out of my grasp
And like the tide
You draw me in
But I know I cannot stay
You are the moon
Mystery and beauty
Silent and distant
Alone in the sky
As you travel round the world
Restless
And you found me
And I feel your pain
It's reflected in me
And I'll always be here for you
But you are not mine
You belong with the stars
As they belong with you
Yet you're so far apart
That we're close in comparison

Though you are separated
Your love is still there
I can see it
It reflects in my eyes
Though you like me
You love him
And you may not know it yet
But until you do
And after
I'll always be here for you
For a time I can keep you whole
But never for long
As you go through phases
Through stages of grief
One day I hope you'll be together again
Be full again
Happy again
And when you smile
The stars wink back
You are the moon
And he is your star
And
I am the sea

I am the moon

I am the moon
Silent and sorrowful
Alone as I hang in the sky
Now I drown in the sea of your eyes
You're the calm and the clear
I'm the bitter salt and the storm
But together we dance
Under the veil of the night
It's written in the stars
You catch my tears
You are the sea.

I am the stars

I am the stars
Scattered in pieces
Shattered in pieces
Woven into the tapestry of the night
You are the moon
You make me whole again
Or as whole as I can be
The meaning of
I love you to the moon and back
Has never been more clear.

You are the stars

You are the stars
You light up my life
Like you light up the night
As you adorn the sky
Like flickering fairy lights
You're eyes sparkle
Like the jewels
Your mind decorated me in
When you tell me I'm beautiful
Your words dance
Round my mind
Scattering my thoughts
Like golden glitter
Your fingers trace patterns
Across my cheeks
Connecting my freckles
Like constellations
Star crossed lovers
Had never made
Much sense
Till now.

The Hungry Dragon

Hiding in the trees, in a deep, dark wood
A hungry young dragon on a hilltop stood
Sick of eating berries and wanting a treat
What he must craved now was some juicy meat!
His stomach made a sound and he rubbed his tummy
Those villagers he thought will taste so yummy.
So in the dead of night whilst the people slept
Down the hill he quietly crept
But what the poor creature
Did not know
The folks weren't ready to be eaten
No no no…
They'd set some traps just in case
Any mean old dragon should show his face
The dragon crept further and down he fell
Splash! Deep inside a cold wet well.
He flapped his wings and flew back out
"I didn't expect that!" he snorted with a pout
Yet he ventured on, until he reached a shed
"They'll be flesh in here" he hopefully said
As he went inside he had such a surprise
When down fell some tools straight into his eyes
The dragon was sad and wanted his mummy
But a rumbling sound still rose from his tummy

He struggled on cautiously to the next farm
Surely there was nothing here to do him harm?
Alas, he was wrong and he let out a wail
As a horse, with big hooves, stamped on his tail
"Ouch!" screeched the dragon as he turned and fled
"I've had enough!" he miserably said
He grabbed some berries and went back to his
Cave
He snuggled in bed not feeling so brave
Huh he thought I'm stick of trying to scare them
"I think I'll become a ….. VEGETARIAN!!!!!"

EYFS

"You work in the EYFS? " They say
But that's just easy, all they do is play!
No times tables or difficult proses,
Isn't it just cleaning & wiping their noses!?
I smile politely, for if only they knew!
Just how much us practitioners really do….

These little people we are preparing
Important ways like "sharing is caring"
How to put on their coats and tie their shoes
How to wash their hands and use the loos
Showing them how to interact and explore
To count, to write, to paint and to draw
To be a good friend and use a kind voice
To sit still on the carpet and make the right
choice
To listen to the teacher and know when to speak
To learn the months of the year and days of the
week
To build a den out of blankets and look after pets
To role play mums & dads, shops and vets
Measuring in water and weighing in sand
Knowing the difference between their right and
left hand
Sharing news and learning to speak out loud

Celebrating achievements in assembly infront of
a crowd
To use scissors safely and hold a pen right
To know the answer is NEVER ever to fight
To learn about reading and their ABCs
But also how to climb and swing on trees
And how to spread butter correctly on bread
To build and plant and bake and thread
To try new foods and pour from a jug
To use kind hands to clap and to hug
To use a saw and hammer a nail
To be resilient - no such thing as to fail
Sorting out quarrels and fallouts with friends
Teaching "I'm sorry" and making a mends
Discussing their feelings be it happy or sad
Knowing stamping on insects is definitely bad
Giving out cuddles when they're feeling low
When they're missing their sister or mum or dad
so
Learning how to form letters and use a full stop
How to run and jump and skip and hop
How to throw and catch and kick a ball
How to crouch down low and stretch up tall
How to roast a marshmallow on an open fire
To make an obstacle course with planks and a
tyre
How to roll sausages and make balls with dough
Encouraging them always just to have a go
How to be independent and keep preserving

Getting the bucket - quick- when they feel like
heaving
Cleaning up cuts and preventing disasters
Going through millions and millions of plasters!
Teaching dance and learning new songs
Helping them know their rights from their
wrongs
Giving out stickers and making them smile
Sitting with a book under a tree for a while
Sharing a story and talking about setting
Labelling possessions cos parents kept
forgetting!
Playing with cars, and dinosaurs (a lot!) The
ability to think of new games on the spot
Sparking imaginations and an enquiring mind
These are just some of the things you will find
A Reception teacher do almost everyday
So no, it's not true, they don't just "play"
Still think it's an easy job to do?
I'm sorry but that's just simply not true!
But would I swap it, absolutely not!
(Even though the pay is really not a lot)
It's such a privilege watching them grow
So for that reason I'll never go
There's never a dull moment it's simply the best
To make a difference in their young lives
I'm definitely blessed.